OCEAN *of* CLOUDS

OCEAN *of* CLOUDS

Poems

Garrett Hongo

ALFRED A. KNOPF

NEW YORK 2025

A BORZOI BOOK

FIRST HARDCOVER EDITION

PUBLISHED BY ALFRED A. KNOPF 2025

Published by Alfred A. Knopf, a division of Penguin Random House LLC,
1745 Broadway, New York, NY 10019.

Knopf, Borzoi Books, and the colophon
are registered trademarks of Penguin Random House LLC.

Library of Congress Cataloging-in-Publication Data
Names: Hongo, Garrett Kaoru, [date] author.
Title: Ocean of clouds : poems / Garrett Hongo.
Description: First edition. | New York : Alfred A. Knopf, 2025.
Identifiers: LCCN 2024028678 | ISBN 9780593802038 (hardcover) |
ISBN 9781524712624 (trade paperback) | ISBN 9780593802045 (eBook)
Subjects: LCGFT: Poetry.
Classification: LCC PS3558.O48 O24 2025 | DDC 814/.54 [B]—dc23/eng/20240624
LC record available at https://lccn.loc.gov/2024028678

penguinrandomhouse.com | aaknopf.com

Printed in Canada
2 4 6 8 9 7 5 3 1

The authorized representative in the EU for product safety and compliance is
Penguin Random House Ireland, Morrison Chambers,
32 Nassau Street, Dublin D02 YH68, Ireland,
https://eu-contact.penguin.ie.

For Charles Wright,

fabbro di stelle e ombre di stelle

Dolce color d'orïental zaffiro,
che s'accoglieva nel sereno aspetto
del mezzo, puro infino al primo giro,

a li occhi miei ricominciò diletto,
tosto ch'io usci' fuor de l'aura morta
che m'avea contristati li occhi e 'l petto.

—DANTE, *Purgatorio*, I, 13–18

Contents

OCEAN *of* CLOUDS

Prologue **I GOT HEAVEN**

I swear that, in Gardena, on a moonlit suburban street,
There are souls that twirl like kites lashed to the wrists of the living
And spirits who spiral in a solemn limbo between 166th
And the long river of stars to Amida's Paradise in the West.

As though I belonged, I've come from my life of papers and exile
To walk among these penitents at the Festival of the Dead,
The booths full of sellers hawking rice cakes and candied plums,
All around us the rhythmic chant of *ondo* bursting through loudspeakers,
Calling out the mimes and changes to all who dance.

I stop at a booth and watch a man, deeply tanned from work outdoors,
Pitching bright, fresh quarters into blue plastic bowls.
He wins a porcelain cat, a fishnet bag of marbles, then a bottle of *shōyu*,
And a rattle shaped like a tam-tam he gives to a child.

I hear the words of a Motown tune carry through the gaudy air
    . . . got sunshine on a cloudy day . . . got the month of May . . .
As he turns from the booth and re-enters the River of Heaven—
These dancers winding in brocades and silk sleeves,
A faithlit circle briefly aswarm in the summer night.

I

UNDER THE OAKS AT HOLMES HALL,
OVERTAKEN BY RAIN

A desert downpour in early spring,
and I'm standing under California oaks,
gazing through rain as the grey sky thunders.
I don't know why the nightingale sings
to Kubla Khan and not to me, nineteen
and marked by nothing, not even ceremony
or the slash of wind tearing through trees.
I don't know why Ishmael alone is left
to speak of the sea's great beast, why
the ground sinks and slides against itself,
why the blue lupines will rise and quilt
through the tawny grasses on the hillsides.
I can't explain this garment of rain on my shoulders
or the sour cloth of my poverty unwinding
like a shroud as the giant eucalyptus
strips and sheds its grey parchments of skin
and stands mottled and nude in the shining rains.
I want something sullen as thundering skies,
thick as earthmilk, brown and sluicing
across the streets, grievous as the flood of waters.
I want unfelt sorrows to give away and wrought absence
to exchange for the imperfect shelter of these oaks,
for the froth of green ivy around my feet,
for the sky without gods and the earth without perplexity.
I want to have something like prayer to pay
or a mission to renounce as a fee
for my innocence under cloud-cover
and these furious nightingales of thunder,
companions of song in this untormented sea
of memory uncrowded with bliss or pain.

READING MIGUEL HERNÁNDEZ
IN BERT MEYERS' LIBRARY

A room surrounded by wooden bookshelves, slim volumes of poetry
>   with colorful spines,
an arcana not only of knowledge, but of human acts on stages
>   both everyday and unimaginable:
>   peasants planting corn in rows of dry earth,
a prisoner being buried whose poems were scratched in blood
>   on his own clothes,
a fisherman who sings to his nets as he sets them out in patches
>   on a shallow sea,
a sybarite sauntering through a Parisian park, scorning the bronze statuary,
a mother grieving at the impassive gates of tyranny, her son
>   disappeared by police.

I learned reverence for the quiet actions of the mind,
>   those who inscribed precise, passionate words
>   onto the chambers of remembrance within languages,
brogues and patois, creoles and chimeras of speech, rhythmic jungles
>   traversed by the resolute beasts of peace.

I read Miguel, Aimé, Sappho, Nâzim, Anna and Cesare.
>   I ate of earth, drank of ice,
saw with eyes tutored by weeping, my body swayed to the cycling music
>   of eternities.
I read to arrive as my teacher saw me, cleansed of cares, swollen heart
>   ready to mourn, tuned to the old music.

SONNY STITT AT THE LIGHTHOUSE, HERMOSA BEACH, 1970

I'd go alone nights to the wide street that led to Hermosa Pier
         and the dark, sighing Pacific beyond.
I'd park a couple blocks away, on a hilly street by the Dari-Mart
And stalk down to the club, a dive with a $6 cover and two-drink minimum
         that let minors in so long as you paid.
I did and heard the greats of the time blasting from the bandstand,
Bending the melodies of tunes I barely knew,
                            playing off the beat sometimes,
counting not the house with a peep from their eyes during a long solo,
but on inspiration to take hold and lift us all from our small oblivions
                            up to the starlit, holy spheres.
They'd start with something from the American songbook
                  or what's called "a standard,"
a love ballad played achingly slow. Then, after a chorus or two you recognized,
a soloist would stretch out, improvising, adding variations, leaving off some notes,
beginning to explore the harmonic pieties of a different order than the straight tune,
exposing its implications, taking from its plainer statements
                            the convoluted harmonic logic implied,
the freer, algorithmic forms emerging from its carnal fundamentals in melody.
It was both abstruse and rootsy in these ways, the thrilling excursions of the solos
always circling back to the plain statement of the initiating vamp, the tune's "head."

I'd heard of Stitt as a bebop pioneer, the man who took Bird's alto style
         and brought it to the tenor, giving it something of his own.
But, when the man walked in, slow and gimp-legged crossing the stage,
I felt pity, a strange and intimate residue of awe transubstantiated.

Stitt had hair like white cotton, a greying moustache drooping
         around the faint scowl on his lips,
and wore a purple shirt that was so tight, he'd unbuttoned it to mid-chest,
exposing a panel of sagging flesh behind the green lanyard for his ax.
The rest of his ensemble was a pair of brown gabardine slacks,
         tan shoes, and a heather sport coat freshly pressed
and so big it hung more like a cape, loose around his frame.

"I've been sick a while," he told us, a small crowd—
        a couple dozen in a space that took a hundred.
"Pneumonia. But I'm gonna try to make it fer ya."

His shoulders sashayed to settle in the space inside the coat
as he wrapped himself around his gleaming instrument
and blew, working its pearly keys with pliant fingers.

Tune after unrecognizable tune came then, lugubriously,
with big, honking notes that sounded like blues with a bad stutter.
When he stopped to twist his mouthpiece
        or to wipe his brow with a big handkerchief,
someone yelled "Play *Mr. Bojangles*!"
        and did it again between every song.

Stitt stopped the set and leaned back in his chair,
        staring into space, his eyes working in slow orbits.
        "I'm sorry I made that record," he snapped,
"with that green bowler on my head, those damn spats on my shoes . . ."

When I spun the LP later, its sound was middlebrow and plainly melodic,
        a step above A&M but just as simple,
its cover art a photo that made of Stitt's elder status a kind of carnival figure,
        genial and welcoming,
displacing the *gravitas* of his history with a cartoon image instantly,
                                        falsely agreeable.
Mr. Bojangles . . . Mr. Bojangles . . . dance . . . the song lyrics say,
                achingly nostalgic about a prior order,
        a subaltern artistry meant only to please.

I intuited his scorn was legit—and I deferred.
He was a *kupuna* of jazz, a *kumu mele*,
        and I've since felt the same,
society preferring my caricature to *the real* of any being.
"Bad for gr/lass . . ." the bumptious Asian gardener says to Nicholson
                                in Polanski's *Chinatown*,
        a spoof on his accent that turns the plot.
        And my own rage is taken as a silly thing, comedic,
impotent as the Chinaman in Nicholson's racist joke.

Stitt turned on the request. "I'll play *How High the Moon,*" he said
                                          and ripped that tune apart,
taking the chords to their outer reaches in bebop speed
                             and angularities of progression.
It lifted us from our small oblivions up to the starlit spheres,
an Empyrean of improvisations emerging from its plain melody.

When it was over, Stitt had slayed us into silence and said,
"Now I'll play a ballad," looking around to his sidemen.
"How 'bout *'Round Midnight?*" said the man on bass,
and they took up the mood, playing like gods,
                          stately in their own space,
the air and audience syncopated around them,
              droning with the bowed strings a lasting part of it.

ON A PHOTOGRAPH OF
CIVIL RIGHTS DEMONSTRATORS

A man wearing a sandwich board walks within a throng.
Across the board's face and back, bold letters read "I AM A MAN."
He feels a change is going to come and it won't be long.

With two hundred others, he protests to right a grave wrong,
Unfair pay for those thought less than men—he took a stand.
Since Dred Scott, our country's laws had kept them down.

Were they born by the river, as in Sam Cooke's gentle song?
Were they running ever since? Does no one give a damn?
Do you, like them, feel a change is gonna come? That it won't be long?

Since Dred Scott, our country's laws had kept them down.
There had been riots, assassinations, the war in Vietnam.
When you see them, do you feel righteous or do you frown?

In '66, I saw the man on television. This happened when I was young.
From then on I worried our policies were all a scam.
Yet, moved by him, I believed a change was gonna come.

Back then, there were times I felt I couldn't last for long.
Now, I glance at this photograph that says I can.
I feel a change is gonna come and that it won't be long.
A man wearing a sandwich board walked within a throng.

THE NIGHT'S CASCADE

Lunch breaks, summer I was 19 clerking for the City, I'd sit on marble benches
across from the glass palace of DWP, over at the Mark Taper,
a theater-in-the-round, eat my sack lunch of sandwich and chips,
and read a book—*Leaves of Grass, The Voice That Is Great Within Us*. . . .
It was hot, upper 80s, the air particled with smog that made an opaque scrim
if you gazed down Dewap and Fig to the distant hills above Chavez Ravine.

I'd lie down and feel the marble under me, let angers drain from my body
as the stone lifted its arms and cold thighs, wresting anguish away.
Once, after a long time lying still as a cadaver, diffuse sun washing over me,
I thought back a half-dozen years to the first time I'd been there, taken
with other boys my age, me alone Japanese, and first heard a magisterial language:

> *Sirs, I am sixty years old. I have lived all my life*
> *Like a wild beast in hiding. Without child, without wife.*
> *People forget me like the mist on Monkey Mountain.*

"Bring two dollars and a sack lunch," Quincy said through his missing front teeth,
dreadlocks dangling to frame his face. "We goin' to see a play by a Caribbean brother."

About twelve of us, bloods and a Buddhahead at the Watts Writers' Workshop,
were carted by bus, 103rd St. to downtown, Four Tops on our transistors—
"Baby, I *need* your loving . . ." as we swayed and rolled our hands, mimicking
moves the Tops made as they crooned "*Got* to have *all* . . . *Oowhoo ooo.* . . ."

We made it to the Music Center, filed out, $2 matinee, got second-row seats;
lights going dim, then dark, and a spot fell on the white disc of an African drum,
then a luminous moon floated over a volcano, soft CO_2 fog creeping onto the stage.
A woman pranced. Then a tall man in a top hat and frock coat, his face half-white
                                                                            with makeup.
They gyrated, then spider danced, weaving their hands, and a voice rose,
the rich Caribbean patois, a creole of English I'd never heard,
and yet understood. It was chanting, chanting . . .

"Ooo, it's the Uncola Man! The Uncola Man!"
someone down the row whispered and was shushed, then a soft billow of light
tumbled its fingers through a cataract of glitter across the rise of voices

and the moon.

Sirs, make a white mist
In the mind; make that mist hang . . .
                    . . . like the breath of the dead . . .

It was a dream and I was in it, back as a boy in fields of cane by the sea again,
weeping for that memory at fourteen, the sound and strophes of my own demesne
reaching, even now, through tides and shallows glittering with the night's cascade
I still wear as a mantle of stars and warm rain dancing me into the next silver decade.

In the college dorm room, I sit cross-legged on the floor,
Scripting ideograms on notebook pages,
Practicing *kanji*, sipping Mateus from a teacup
Blazed with coppery red dragons with golden eyes.
Barefoot, I wear jeans and a plain white tee,
And bend from the waist to do this steady work.
Motown plays from the stereo—the Temps
Crooning a cool tune—and a rhythm slowly builds,
A sinuous pulse of wordless feeling, a guide for phrasing,
And the images rise, recollections from childhood,
The scents of the past, the chant of tides from the sea,
A garland of cigarette smoke curling through household air,
My grandfather dealing flower cards before him on the floor:
The first plum blossoms bursting from a black bough,
Yellow butterflies ringed around peonies, a white heron
Poised between twin pines before a pink cascade of *sakura*.
Legacy is like this—insinuations, stray images
Collecting in the mind stilled from passion,
Fundaments persisting in our waking dreams.
I move the cup aside, shimmering with wine.
Left to right, I gather strophes with a pen,
From a swirl of flowers, trail of ideograms . . .
Running away with me . . . tell you, once again . . .

AFTER WORKSHOP, LATE FALL

In Balboa, waiting for the ferry,
Mike and I dockside at coffee, Yusef
And Jones in the Volks with Elaine and Andy . . .
From the car's AM, *I Can't Help Myself*
Cut through the light smog, chased all our worries.
The waitress brought Mike a latté—half-caff.
An oil slick from a yacht or small dory
Spread rainbows on the water, an aleph

Curving toward us, a moment's chance to see
What conjures it might bring—a map of stars,
An apparition in evening's black coffee,
Jump-starts, a flicker from gods in palm trees
Wicking down to us like fire, in idling cars,
Blood moon on the channel's blue sleeve of sea.

HOMAGE TO MICHAEL S. HARPER
AT THE EQUINOX OF HEAVEN

The frozen white humps and hillocks of your Providence landscape
Seem to me the extended reef of dead coral in a silted bay,
Brown skeletons of winter trees like the fronds of fan and finger coral
Reaching through a flurry of diatoms for the surface of the sea.
But those are snowflakes tracking our passage from the airport
Where you'd just met me curbside, pointing to my bare head,
Saying *You gots to have some kinda hat in this shit,* pulling off
The grey and black Nigerian fez and waving it like a hook
Through the frozen air. You fling my luggage into the trunk
Of your maroon, 5-speed Saab, and we're off, blasting Coltrane's
Naima on the 5-channel, custom surround-sound of your car stereo.

Your rap peppers the air, a non-stop, soul-soliloquy you whistle
Through a gap-toothed, Cab Calloway smile that disappears into
Disquisitions on male fashion, critiques of my green L.L. Bean polo,
Instructing me that *You just can't wear no argyle socks . . .*
Banners of earthly wisdom tailing into the common stream
Of celestial harmonies emanating from Tyner's keyboard
As he comps on your words chattering like a snare and hi-hat
                                        chomping on the beat.

You don't take me to my hotel but to your loft home instead,
A 2nd-floor walkup through a wide stairway, behind a solid,
Metal door with three locks and a numbers code you punch in,
Saying with a grin, *It's the same ol' three-six-nine.*

It's a tri-level with cantilevered bedrooms, a sunken kitchen,
And a big living space filled with two couches, a tv on a rolling stand,
Huge museum-sized paintings hung above a long, low bookcase
That stretches across the length of the room, full of record albums,
All *Periodized, alphabetized, and absolutely no fusion allowed.*
"Closest we git is Rufus and Chaka Khan," you confess.

You've a turntable and slide a white-jacketed LP out of its sleeve.
A surprise, you say, flipping it to the choice A-side
And settling its cutout eye onto the silver spindle.
The bassline jumps into the long vamp of a hardass hook,
And the air comes alive with a dance beat, synth notes
Jumping our bones as you bob your head, *The hardest thing to move,*
As your ample body shakes to the rhythm and you slap on the One,
The plain white cover of the album flapping against heavy gabardine—
Small explosions of cloth billowing your shivering pant leg
As Jackson coos and screams. It's *Billie Jean*, first I ever heard it,
Its prehensile sound moonwalking across your loft's hardwood floor.

sex fingers toes there is no substitute for pain
        you tuck the roots in the earth

At the faculty club, you show me how to cut the yellow flowers
                                        of frozen butter,
Break bread in pieces before the silver paddle of the knife touches them.
We talk about your roots in Brooklyn before your parents moved West
To Crenshaw in L.A., your Japanese neighbors, the stain of Camp
                                        still on their souls.
Bloods and Buddhas schooling each other, rice and Rasta
                        on the dance floor at Dorsey High,
Motown and *min'yō* our common mix-tape,
                        Can't nobody take it apart . . .

Back in Iowa City, there for the Workshop, you and Inada
                        couldn't rent a room,
so Rutsala fooled the landlord, got the lease, and you two moved in.
Three months until December and then eviction *for some bullshit,*
Your poems in praise of jazz greats in boxes on the street outside,
Gathering a dust of snow.

            The inflated heart the tenor kiss

At the reading, you spoke of Robert Hayden murmuring on his death bed
Words that still burn in my ears, and I read a poem from a photograph
"On Civil Rights Demonstrators," water cannons on the Edmund Pettus Bridge,
"I AM A MAN," and three from *The Dartmouth Review* rose from where they sat

On the carpeting of that fine, book-lined library room, buttoned up their coats,
And walked out mid-poem, a needle of ice running through my heart.

> *why you so funky?*

cause I am
> *why you so black?*

cause I am

Who knows that Isherwood was your early mentor?
That Auden came to class and praised your poems?

> *cause I am*

How far have we come with history as our own heartbeat?

Minstrelsy   Yellowface   Rochester and Hop Sing

Kin is more than a cold word spoken on frozen stairs.

your body now crystal as *you plod up into the electric air*
heart, genitals, and sweat

Dear Michael . . .
> *why you so sweet?*

cause I am cause I am

The dawn comes upon both of us, rising in the east,
Providence to L.A., a sun caught in the coral fingers of a tree

by river through the swamps witness to   *a love supreme*

WATCHING TURNER CLASSICS WITH STANLEY CROUCH AT THE HEBREW HOME, RIVERDALE

I've come from a continent away to your semi-private room
at the Hebrew Home here in Riverdale-on-the Hudson.
I'm told Wynton has provided for you, that your ex- still comes
every other week, bringing news and fussing you, that you speak
but your timing's off, slowed, that you still talk girls but slurred.

I come in homage, to see an elder, my mentor in jazz and arrogance,
the man who taught me fight was love sometimes, leather was cool,
shades was cooler, that blood rules a heavy step, your muscular tread
shaking the floorboards with each cock-of-the-walk strut
up the aisle of a theater, you arriving late, commanding attention,
barking out the rules of a Black aesthetic, a carny or cornerman
with his bandages and spit cup, patching up the pain, cuts, and wounds
with words from Langston Hughes.

                              You spoke with the rhythms,
melodies of the barbershop, your argumentative stance
demanding drama in any voice that may have started with a rasp
but then elevated into soft strophes like Lester's saxophone
flowing a sideways tune, lifting his ax near horizontal,
a smooth sashay of persuasion, streetcorner sophistry that convinced
light was from gods and liberation came from words.

Cinqué, Amistad, Benito Cereno, Poeta en Nueva York
I first heard you say, who told me *A black man a white one*
look the same down a street in Harlem a hundred yards away.
They both have the rhythm of jazz in their step, the beat
of the street, the same pace, the flavor of motion, you said.
Or they'd both be dead. It's culture that brings us the game.
It's bullshit mounds us apart. We are sons of Cain,
one and the same, Holmes, and seek a mutual, ancestral heart.

"Post-war, it was television and movies pushed the Afro-American
to demand de-segregation," you suddenly state, your eyes
still on the tv screen, where Barbara Stanwyck in salon curls
washes dishes in her kitchen, and Fred MacMurray in a suit,
his hat cocked back, dandles a cigarette, *noir*ish, from his lips.
He sat at her table, a newspaper in his hands, clueless
as everyday, humdrum, at a point before the fatal kick of the plot.
"Afro-Americans could see another way, moving pictures the revelation,
and they wanted it, got off sharecroppin' and moved they ass north.
It was tv started us on the path to *Brown v. Board of Education*."

Then you spun out a chorus of classic riffs, extended tropes
and filigrees of rhetoric ornamenting your speech, a shattered voice
rising to an airy tenor range before you quit, your eyes gone flat,
you suddenly stone silent as I stood by, heart-kicked, amazed like that.

II

ORISON: FEBRUARY, EUGENE, OREGON

for Al Young

Months of heavy rain and the back lawn
                                   is an emerald pond
with islands of fig and apple trees and their dirt collars
darkening under the pixilated grey of a computer screen sky.

I've cinched my desires in a handful of thin books,
wired the dwarf pines and maples in their pots on the deck
and instructed them in *Soul Train* and break-dance poses
to beguile my children and signify what's past.

Which is various: Motown and *min'yō* blaring together
                              on the PA of my high school gym,
emanations of soul and *shamisen* from the living room stereo
back when I was a child, Sam Cooke's *A Change Is Gonna Come*
rising like a willow tree by a smooth-flowing river
banded with a long slick of stars streaking across its back
in a wall-hanging of calligraphy and gaudy prints
                                   over the Silvertone console.

I tell myself I've drifted too far now to go back,
my *karma* the boat of a dry leaf caught in the swirls of that river
taking me from ghetto to this immaculate garden
                              without stain or confusion,
everything so calm and forgotten, the anguish I have
like the darting squirrel that emerges, a nervous
                                   and comic thing,
unavailed of all the refulgence and splendor that surrounds him
and would inspire a lapse from instinct and pain
if not for the immutable worry
that jags through his heart like a dance.

TO MY STUDENTS IN CRWR 330,
WINTER 2017

Among my students, I feel alone with history,
my past so hard won and assembled from bits of story
passed among the elder relatives sipping Old Fashioneds
                                         on holidays,
legs crossed and sitting on *zabuton* on the floor,
winners raking in their chips from a poker game
or losers tossing *hanafuda* cards aside
with a satiric curse *Gunfunnit, I stay make* . . .

And theirs carefully pieced too,
                       full of internet frivolity,
Twittersphere feeds, YouTube videos, and TikTok jingles,
the past a *Lucy Show* or the photograph
of their parents on their wedding day
I ask them to find and describe to me.

They look at it and cannot keep the pronouns straight—
You for when they mean *I, They* when
they want to say *My beloved prarodičě in Brno* . . .

It's hard for them to enter the past,
                    so they abstract themselves
out of their perfect bodies and thrift store clothes,
their Lands' End shoes and jeggings of faux leather.
They cannot say *I gaze at your face in wonder*
but declare that prickle of feeling attributes to another—
that *You* who sits over a tablet screen at Starbuck's,
sipping a latté, slowly, as though there were no time
and heaven surrounds us already, an absence
that disavows beginnings, makes us each

an anonymous light in a constellation of the undefined,
that *vajra* a flame-shaped luminance like a tear
staining the edges of an old photograph
that you slip out of your wallet and tuck back in
before anyone can see that you've looked,
that your face has grown into its own character.

A GARLAND OF LIGHT

to the memory of Robert Hayden

I had taken a long walk from my hotel near the Colosseum
past the antique earth colors of ruins at the Forum
down busy, traffic-laden streets to the Trevi Fountain,
its lip ringed with throngs of tourists snapping selfies—
a father bending to the waters and cupping his hands
to offer his toddler son a cool drink amidst the glister—
sculptures of the gods serene but spouting an abundance
that lapped gorgeously over carved stone to the brilliant,
pooling fan that made this upwelling a semicircle of the bucolic.
I moved through to a kind of winding approach to the Steps
and descended, picking through the patches of crowds
huddled in an angling shade cast by the Keats-Shelley House.

On the street before the fountaining Bernini boat in the piazza,
I button-hooked into the entrance and climbed wooden stairs,
paid my fee to the smiling attendant, and entered the sacred rooms:
a kind of library with long walls lined with books, busts of Keats
and Shelley, glass cases of miscellaneous manuscripts,
wispy locks of their tawny hair, other small trinkets of their lives.
In Severn's room, the small chamber adjacent to where Keats died,
I found a printed card and read the words of Charles Cowden Clarke,
Keats' boyhood friend, telling how, after the poet had left Enfield School
to apprentice to an apothecary at a village two miles away,
they'd still meet, "five to six times a month," Keats with book in hand,
so they might sit at an arbor at the edge of a spacious garden
to while away a leisure hour with "good talk" of *The Faerie Queen*
"to note the spark that fired the train of his poetical tendencies . . ."

But a reflection on the glass shone through the translucency of years—
a frosted flame of thought that took me back through the inactive pages of my life—
and I was humbled to recall my own student time—22 in Ann Arbor,
fresh from Japan and my monastery year—sitting with Robert Hayden in his garden.
It was fall term and I'd pursued him, asking for conference hours.

He dismissed all my suggestions and simply said, "We shall read Keats,"
inviting me to have tea every Monday afternoon at his house.
I'd ride a borrowed woman's Schwinn, my books in a wicker basket,
and he'd be there reading on his porch, rising to greet me
like a streetlamp looming over autumn blossoms, Coke-bottle
glasses gleaming at their rims, red or yellow bow-tie at his wrinkled neck,
the white dress shirt flapping lightly in the breezes like drying laundry,
his hair Brilliantined and scented with a light, floral trace.

I never took one note, instead listened intently to his pure voice,
murmuring the great lines
            . . . as though of hemlock I had drunk,
    Or emptied some dull opiate to the drains
            One minute past and Lethe-wards had sunk . . .
                In some melodious plot
            Of beechen green, and shadows numberless . . .
while the garden swam in flurries of light around us—
white gladiolas, tumbles of trumpet blossoms, a vine of wisteria
yet to bloom snarling over a dingy trellis shading the gate.

He taught me rhythm, phrasing, attention for metaphor,
the organic and spectral weave of syntax coiling to simile,
design all in shadow until the burst that reveals the shining figure
alit with clarified thought:
    O, for a draught of vintage! that hath been
        Cool'd a long age in the deep-delved earth,
    Tasting of Flora and the country green,
        Dance, and Provençal song, and sunburnt mirth!
The man who, in his own poems, told of slave ships, rebellions,
great leaders of his race—El-Hajj Malik El-Shabazz—
chronic angers and love's austere and lonely offices . . .

What did I know? And did I know that his gift to me
was a mirror of mutual affections refracted through
the burbling Hippocrene from over a century before
when vows once spoke between two friends remain
through *the pastoral eglantine . . . like crimson dyed in grain . . . ?*
He was a man who like a breath ascends amidst the roil of years,
who gave me the utter sound of words like a water-writ script
rolling gently as a garland of light on the swells of a fountain.

AT THE GRAVE OF ANTONIO GRAMSCI, CIMITERO ACATTOLICO, ROMA

He is at the far end of the cemetery,
down a long walk right from the entrance,
then up a short path, then right again.
You'll find his marker, roughened grey stone
with the clean, capital letters of his family name
and dates of life and terrible death (at Quisisana in Rome)
on a smooth field over an olive branch
embossed decorously from the middle right
to near the upper left where an umbrella tree
bursts its green pinwheels of leaves beside it.
Two earthenware pots, empty, rise from the ground
at the foot of the stone surrounded by red blooms of geraniums.

A woman in sports clothes sits on a stair of the pathway
And texts on her smartphone balanced on her bare knee.
No drone of planes, mowers, or leaf blowers—
it's quiet as a church except for the light, digital tapping
dotting the spaciousness of air that descends upon us.

Years ago, I read his *Quaderni del carcere* and understood
that television was a laugh track to oppression, that the angelic orders
of state and society were Erinyes poisonous to my own liberty,
that my voice was to sing of my ancestors' struggle in the canefields.

A man approaches with his toddler son,
but they veer to another gravesite,
and I gather myself, clap twice, and bow,
chant a shard of the Heart Sutra—
gyate, gyate . . . parasamgyate—
for his soul freed of its body, bodhisattva of praxis,
prophet of change borne by the river of stars.

TANZAKU: SEVEN SNAPSHOTS IN ITALY

Orvieto to Firenze

Carousels and their gaudy flickers of light,
    candy-skinned ponies,
the circumference of the world aswirl . . .

From the start you struck poses, voguing,
lifting your arm, torso twisted, *contrapposto*,
an aerialist, barely earthbound . . .

Greve

A bloom of goat's beard big as your face, radiant white starburst,
puffball of Aeoleus and *putti*. . . . Cheeks full of wind like Diz,

you blow and, from the stem in your hand, stars stream,
each a universe, kind of Mnemosyne, parachutes of promise . . .

San Zaccaria

You wear a pea-green Gore-Tex jacket over Gap Kids cottons,
your feet in Mary Janes, and strike a *kabuki* pose,
one leg outstretched, the other bent at the knee,

and I recognize it's a *mie* from *Sukeroku*, your umbrella a peony
blooming over your shoulder as though the Venetian rain
were just layered on a cobblestone street in Osaka.

Duomo

Four years old, you climbed 3,000 stairs with me . . .
the look down from the rim of the bell of the apse . . .
the look up through all the winding murk . . .

until that burst of sunlight and wind
opened to the roofs of the city laid out
like 10,000 scales on a terra-cotta fish.

The Bridge of Sighs

You loved the tale of Casanova diving from the bridge in escape,
        a gondola awaiting him,
its black prow coursing through the lacquer of night,

your smile while crossing the narrow hall, the grin of a goblin,
eyes lit by the brief moon of my camera's flash.

Birthday in Bassano

The glee, fork poised over a plate of squid-ink pasta . . .

Le Giubbe Rosse

Near recumbent on your side, you lounged in the linen seat,
your face becalmed, a Noh mask agaze at the Everlasting.

READING JARMAN AT SHAKESPEARE
AND COMPANY, PARIS, 2017

Warm afternoon sun high and to the right above the rose of the cathedral on Île de la Cité,
the narrow, cobbled street in front of me like a wharf with a flotilla of bistro tables
                                                    and chairs,
the lunch crowd casting off, abandoning its digestifs and ravaged tiramisu,
I hear canticles of churchbells from Notre Dame intermingled with traffic noise—
impatient beeps from horns and the wasplike whine from motor scooters accelerating
                                        into the scrum of buses and cars—
a sonic palette of babble in Shanghai Chinese and French speakers seated alongside me
on the picnic table outside the café of the bookstore patronized by the famed Moderns.
It's a student crowd in early spring—bare-armed young women in blouses
                                        like splashes of paint
in primary colors flouncing over the black of their pencil skirts and leg-hugging slacks,
stubble-faced young men in long-sleeved tees and stone-washed jeans,
every one with a smartphone or Bluetooth mike at their lips like Eucharistic wafers
about to be received and swallowed, body of Apple, bread of Android. . . .
Not a tourist near except a Chinese matron in eggplant slacks and a white linen jacket
walking arm-in-sauntering-arm with her French companion, herself dressed
                                        in a suit of rose-colored silk.
Wilco-Tango-Foxtrot, everybody looks so damn cool as though already in a painting
                                        by Pissaro at Musée d'Orsay.
My daughter, jet-lagged, is asleep in our tiny, fourth-floor hotel room in Rive Gauche
(I've left a note, tucked into her suede boot beside the bed, that I'm around the corner),
and I've come to read my friend's poetry, a new book he gifted me with last December
                                        in LA's Venice.
"After a year of too much face time," Jarman writes in "The Heronry," the title poem
composed from a bluff overlooking a coastal estuary rich with bugs and birdlife,
he came so he could "gaze across the face of a lagoon" and "out over the shallows,
near where a black phoebe fluttered and looped . . . and the night herons
                                        studied their dreams."
For me too, it's been months since my time was my own, days filled with worry
                                        and obligations,
the trivial importances of an academic life and the burden of my own soullessness
                                        as I've lived it.

"Simply to watch as other creatures lived . . . lent me a greater peace than prayer,"
the poet tells me, and I know for myself that the way is non-contention
                                                    and yet I've contended,
lived by opposition rather than a righteous surrender. I've thought myself virtuous,
pono, as the Hawaiians say, a scowl on my brow every day, blasphemies on my tongue
as though truculence and self-tyrannizing might lift the world and an angry heart
like a roseate sun held with tenderness against the baptismal bowl of sky.
Follow the breath, a teacher once told me, let the leaf gather what the world sends
in spirals of a spiritless wind that asks questions of no one who lies down
on his left or right side, whose eyes brim at the gateless gate like chalices of wine.

The Big (double-deck) Bus exhales its pneumatic brakes at the curb
                                                    of Rue Saint-Julien-le-Pauvre,
and the swank tables of Quai de Montebello fill and refill around me like cups of americano
or, better still, caffè macchiato topped with tulips of milk and the white whips
                                                    of a delicate sentience.

ANNALENA STARING INTO THE SUN, KOAIʻA TREE SANCTUARY, HAWAIʻI

We'd started amidst woodside clumps of cactus, bearded with soft, yellow spines,
wind whipping at our backs as we climbed through grass and scrub
                                        and passed a sentinel *ʻie ʻie*
to pause within a waist-high grove of acacia trees, their branches bouncing,
that briefly sheltered us so we could gaze back at the gentle descent
                                        of the deep, green land
rolling below out towards the grey glint of the sea that shimmered beyond.

Alex stopped and took a picture—Annalena, 12, her brown hair spearing out
                                        in a halo from her head
like you see in the paintings of saints from the quattrocento, rays of light in an aura,
her raincoat blue as the folds of robe in the tondo by Michelangelo,
the roil of landscape spread out like an arcane scroll with its green myths.

She gazed at the yellow zigzag of sun as it broke through an archipelago
                                        of slate clouds
and made a blaze of script over the sentient slope of lava land.
An ampersand or treble clef it seemed, that morphed into *sōsho*—
a sunshower of ideograms—the billowing calligraphy of words for wind
                                        flowing through grasses of a meadow.

BEACHES

Lāʻie

Particles of fine beach sand the color of *café au lait*
                                        spackled to our skins,
my daughter, 4, and I raise up when we see it—
a baby monk seal lying on its side at the curve of the bay,
dark, sea-worn rocks like a pod of them
had just washed ashore, skins sparkling,
the curling onrush from the sea bathing them
                        in foam and ribbons of *limu*
as though a mother were soaping her children with
                                a sudsy, green cloth.

But there is no movement, no flesh stirring
                                under the folds of skin,
and the eyes don't blink, glaucous stare from them
agaze at the nothing beyond the three of us
gathered in wonder, in worship for the life to come.

Kaimu

We parked the rental on a hillock surrounded by black lava fields,
stepped out, and felt the onshore breeze surge through our clothes.

We walked through scrub *ʻōhiʻa* and baby coconut palms,
their fronds sprouting like green tentacles in the wind,

and climbed a final bluff, mounded reds of *ʻaʻā* cut by a stream
                                of silvery *pāhoehoe*
we followed as our route through to the sea, blue curls of surf

sighing into black sands, skirts of white frothing at the shore,
horizon a slate line under the beryl ocean of clouds.

With Mahealani Pai

Bare-chested, barefoot, he strides atop the rockwall
of Kaloko-Honōkahau and points to the curling wave
stitched with streaks of *āholehole* racing through its glassy face,
a gorgeous, heaving miracle on the breast of the earth
freckled with darts of light like silvery daybreaks,

like dozens of mele moons.

Wai'ōpae Tidepools

Silhouetted against the silver-grey screen of sky,
Alex, my oldest, wades through the still pond,
picking his way over black stones and the broken

hummocks of lava worn by the sea

to where there's depth enough to swirl, pivoting,
buoyed in a silva-tint of waters, his fanlike hands weaving
through a sticky light, soft susurrus of wind that holds him
suspended in the aqueous stretch of a scalloped planet.

Vada

The soft death rattle of smooth grey stones at the shore,
the shallow stink of the sea, froth of tides, dirty hems of the wind . . .
I'm where the 442nd bivouacked by the beach, 1944,
crouching over dinners of K-rations over kindling fires.
One among them recalls a swing tune—Glenn Miller—to console his terror—
temblors from the earth under cannonades of frightful surf.

Divi Bay, Saint Martin

Melancholic yesterday, watching slate-grey clouds
showering down while I lay in a cozy, one-man cabana,
inhabited by fine striations of grief, lamenting a loss.

I thought of writing to the soul of Nâzim Hikmet,
saying loving a woman was like writing a book—
that you must do it every day and not forget

it is love's body on which you write a page of kisses,
turning her over to smooth her shoulders,
rubbing her crease with the blade of your hand.

Then, a sunshower hit and *the silvery alphabet of the sea*
spelled a god's name on the frothy foot to a page of surf.

Punaluʻu

The magical underside of the world,
                         black glass shattered into sands
heaved into the dark spires of each successive wave . . .

Bowl of shadows lined with white curls of froth,
fingers of seawrack wreathed in spume,
baubles of turtles sliding through your grasp,

You heave with the sighs of an invisible moon,
you mount the earth with salty loins,
                         you crest with pyramids of desire,
while indecipherable wisdoms,
                         intoned by each splash of the sea
reach out to us, surging to steal the shoals of our bodies,
to bring to us its barren, black-toothed bite.

Anzio

Narrow shelf of rough beach, short sandstone cliffsides,
Thousands crowded onto the inhospitable shore,
German artillery from the bluffs only a quarter-mile away
Pounding them with the fractured, black shells of death . . .

A platoon of Nisei soldiers waded these waters,
Chest-deep with fear, the blood in their ears
Beating a rhythm, a march, a dirge as they came ashore,
Scream of guns, guts of men scattering in salt air.

WATCHING THE FULL MOON
IN A TIME OF PANDEMIC

I watch the full moon's light slide like silver water through the silhouettes of trees
that cast long shadows over mounds and rocks, a hidden stream, and the expanse of lawn.
I think back to when I played hide-and-seek games with cousins at the shoreline,
Pūpūkea near Shark's Cove on Oʻahu, dodging in and out of the shadows of ironwood trees.

We hid amidst the vapors of murk mixed with sea spray and wild laughter,
sought one another in sands under the glassy moonlight that splashed our bodies like surf.
We stood as though rooted, silent while sighs from the sea carried through cool, night air.

I was four or I was five and I was not Leanne or Neal or Kerry, but myself,
counting my own breath, one with the dark, gazing at the silver gleam of heaven's road
making its path from below the moon across heaving, purple waters to where I stood
as I do tonight, sixty years from that first shining. I told it to my daughter,
who hid in moonshade, isolate and lonely, missing the welter of what life had been,
her father five as a child unfathomable, her slim form disappearing, while I stood, seeking.

HER MAKEUP FACE

Louise Tomiko Hongo, I.M.

There were years at her bedroom vanity, daubing on
makeup, fussing with clips and brushes, a clamp
for eyelashes, the phalanx of powder jars and perfume
bottles assembled like the glassy face of a wave standing
over a box of Kleenex. She'd paint on lipstick,
then blot the excess with a fold of pink tissue pressed
between her lips, pulling pins and a net from her hair,
grabbing up her purse and high-heeled shoes,
almost ready to step up the tiered flights of City Hall stairs
and the long day's work bossing the typists and Clerk IIs.

How long was this her life, composed or grudging amidst
the clatter of machines, the pouches and memos
that swelled like a tide of incoming blather each day
she stood at her desk, commanding Stella Sue from Memphis,
Helena from Jalisco, and Kay (short for Keiko) from Boyle Heights?
How many times must she have thought of flowers floating in a tree,
archipelagos of plumeria buoyed on their branches
as a soft, onshore wind brought the scent of the sea
to the sub-tropical *pietà* of a mother and her newborn,
wrapped in blue flannels, in her arms as she sat on a torn
grass mat on the lawn by the browning litter of blooms
beneath a skeletal tree by a bungalow in Kahuku?

In her last illness, while lying comfortably in her bed
in the semi-private room of the care center in Carson, California,
her mind and lifelong rage sweetened by the calm of forgetfulness,
she said she wanted to go back, that it was "a good place"
and she'd like living there again. "Ripe mangoes and guava taste
every day," she said. "And everybody knows you your family bess."

She spoke in pidgin like this, without demands, no fusillades
of scorn nor admonishments like I'd gotten steadily since childhood—
the torch of discontent that had lit a chronic, rancorous façade
had doused itself in the calm waters of a late life lagoon
that caught her in its tidal fingers and captured her moonlike face
so that, when she gazed upon me those last days,
she did not scowl but smiled, her tyrannous visage
made plain, beatific without blemish of pain or artifice.

IN MARBLE AND LIGHT

Albert Kazuyoshi Hongo, I.M.

I once saw somewhere, in a box of old financials, check-stubs,
and paid bills, or leaned up against a dusty mirror, amidst vials

of nail polish and mascara cluttered on my mother's vanity
table in their bedroom, an old, 8x10 photograph of my father

with two of his war buddies. It was a black-and-white studio shot
touched up so their faces looked like smooth marble, but sepia-

toned with a cast of weak coffee. They wore dress khakis,
smoothly starched shirts with campaign ribbons across their chests,

and a stripe or two on their long, pressed sleeves. My father's
bore none, but his black hair rode up like a glassy wave slicking

over one side of his head, hatless, unlike the others who wore caps.
It must've been when we lived in Midtown L.A., in the apartment house

with a Hawaiian name on South Kingsley Drive when I saw it.
I was six or seven, and he told me he'd been a guard at Nuremburg,

passing Lucky Strikes to S.S. officers imprisoned there
who begged for them before they went on trial.

Zigaretten, bitte, he'd say, his one phrase of German,
and he grinned when he said it, as though it were the cheesiest

joke of his life. He never told me one thing else about the war
except that he'd brought a Luger and a Leica back from there

that my mother made him sell. "She no like war souvenir,"
he said, waving his hand in dismissal. In the fall of 1987,

three years after he died, I went along to a memorial
gathering at Arlington, the National Cemetery, invited there

by my senators from Hawai'i, themselves decorated veterans.
I stood at the top of an amphitheater and gazed down at all

the assembled of the 442nd that day, scores of old men
in their sixties and seventies, grey and shrunken in their

informal aloha clothes, their hair silver under VFW caps.
Dan Inouye, my father's teammate from McKinley High's

football varsity, led me down the shallow steps, saying
"There are some guys I want you to meet." I staggered

obediently along. About halfway, a group of less than a dozen
men stood up as we approached, some reaching to take

the senator's only hand. He slipped it free and gestured
toward me, turning. "This is Al Hongo's boy," he said, simply.

Then, one by one, like mourners at a funeral, each of them
shuffled up and shook my hand, some saying nothing

but looking deep into my eyes, theirs glistening in the autumn light.
One in a wheelchair backed himself out from the end of the aisle—

his hands were in dark half-gloves and I saw trousers rolled up
where his legs might've been. Then he pushed toward me, reaching,

his hands beckoning me to bend toward him. I did, thinking
that he might take the lei of green *ti* leaves from his shoulders

and place it around my neck, that I would be kissed in greeting.
But his hands reached past to my face, and I felt his free fingers

rubbing a soft arpeggio against my cheeks and the hollows above my jaw,
slow strokes as though a dirge were in their touch, cadenced and resolute.

"Your face the same as your father's," he said, the palms of his gloves rough
as emery against my skin. And I was made marble, wet with a shining light.

Memorial Day, 2018
Anzio

III

HOMAGE TO A PICTURE BRIDE

When years were long with labor in the sugarfields,
I sought a wife, at last, choosing her from a photograph.
She was but fifteen, a shy child of a bride
wrapped in faded *kimono*, as I likewise was wrapped in wind,
a man of thirty, weathered by work in the green seas
of cane, my savings finally enough to take my wedding vows.

Before then, it was to the coming world that I made vows
to wrest a new life from the earth and leave the fields
so I might cast my eyes without sorrow from mountains to the sea,
never again to falsify who I was in a photograph
as though I were a clerk or saddler, sheltered from the constant winds,
the image I'd sent, a deception to my young bride.

She was young but daily growing, my new bride.
We stood on the pier and took our vows,
and I led her to the North Shore, its mountains torn by winds,
below them the rippling green fields
of cane stretching all the way to the sea,
a landscape no one would care to photograph.

Before we left, someone took a photograph—
this laborer and downcast picture bride
half his age at their dockside ceremony of vows—
staged before a background of slate-grey seas
and the small curls of waves tossed by winds,
impassive faces resigned to a hard life in the canefields.

So, we were destined never to leave the fields—
my wife gave birth to a son we did not photograph
as, before he could cry, he was taken by the wind
that came betrothed as his own promised bride,
journeying from the Afterworld over storm-tossed seas,
our mortal dreams of a better life all but disavowed.

She herself died within a year of our vows
and so finally escaped the sugarfields,
a ghost in flight, *ha ʻalele hana*, over the dread seas
that never would be captured in a photograph,
so that, ever after, only resolve would be my bride
and my mourning cloak a coat of harsh winds.

Only the wind knows my sorrows now, whatever vows
my bride and I made are forever lost in the sugarfields,
this photograph the one moment we lived apart
                                        from life's cold seas.

KUBOTA TO ZBIGNIEW HERBERT IN LVOV, 1942

In 1942, as Lvov was being seized by Nazis while you labored
diligently by day as a quiet feeder of lice in a virus lab
and joined your heart to the resistance that would rise in Warsaw,
my own country's agents had already taken me from my home in Lā'ie,
placed me in a jail cell in Honolulu, and interrogated me for many days.
Neither of us had thought of our poetry then, Zbigniew,
not of the caustic sarcasm of your strophes stripped of pious words,
not of the praises of the life I would lose like a lavish field of rice
once bending with weight but blighted overnight by the black cowls of disease.
I told them I was just a storekeeper who liked night fishing—no submarines
was I signaling offshore, nothing but schooling fish did I hope would come
to the sputtering lights of my torches that I stuck in the sand like stakes
for growing beans in my family garden. The ocean knew of my intentions,
lapping softly at my knees, curling in kind, foaming waters
around the bones of my bare feet. And the winds knew of my poverty,
sending me a cloudless night sky, stippling the lagoon with stalks of red flames.
But my government questioners cited my language was the enemy's,
my academy in Hiroshima a military school, my citizen's heart black as crude oil.

They sent me to a barracks on an island in Pearl Harbor
where I could see the burnt wreckage of scores of ships,
hear their moaning steel like drowned sailors who still cry out,
throats scorched by burning diesel, from their watery graves,
feel nothing but panic and regret as though a child had died,
my hope wrapped in old newspapers and thrown away like offal
cleaned from a fish the size of a man. Then to a ship bound for Oakland,
and by train and truck with men like me, Japanese all, to Fort Missoula
and a cold wind like a dull razor scraping across my stubbled face.
What was my crime except to belong to an enemy race?
Why can they not see that I love, like them, the promise
that is this land like a wife to whom we have sworn
only faith and practiced devotion? I would wash her feet with water

gathered in a canvas bucket, carry her burdens across canefields
and over the shallows of our bay, ruffled with wind, if she would,
yet once more as on her bridal evening, speak her vows and turn the soft bundles
of her body, heaving like a warm tide in my arms, back to mine.

KUBOTA DISEMBARKS THE SS *LURLINE* IN
OAKLAND, JANUARY 1942

My third sea voyage was not to Japan
or inter-island to scout a new home for my family,
but imprisoned on a ship bound from Honolulu to Oakland,
where I was, once more, placed in handcuffs
before armed guards walked me down the gangplank.

F.B.I. said I was "enemy alien" and fail to register,
but I was born in U.S. like them, on Waialua Plantation.
1899 the records show, but they no bother check,
just grab me up, interrogate me, try trick me,
but I no fall. I give same answer every time—
I night fishing for kumu and the torches not
for signal submarine off the shore, notch a path
for torpedo planes for come December 7th,
but only attract fish for come my net.
They throw me in jail after that, then put me
on the Lurline locked in steerage with Japanee like me—
language teacher, accountant, newspaper reporter,
and even one doctor and one dentist who no talk whole time—
most of us silent as the sea go rock us in our bunks,
only few talking story, most just barely breathing
while the ship engines slowly wormed eastward to the Mainland.

After we docked, we were hustled on deck, handcuffed,
and marched down a gangplank while a news photographer
took pictures with a Graflex, bursts from his flash throwing a white fire
over our shivering bodies, shaming us as soldiers stood around
at the ready, Enfield rifles on their shoulders, helmets on their heads,
waiting to escort us to a truck with its engine running,
diesel fumes in the air, plugs misfiring, body shuddering
like a dog whipping off water after a plunge in the sea.

We walked in a stiff line, heads bowed, trying to hide
our faces for the dishonor we felt, made into criminals overnight

by this war without mercy for us as Japanese,
in their minds no different than the pilots who attacked Pearl.
But we are not warriors. I am a storekeeper
and spent my days counting stock, canned goods, and sundries,
figuring sums and sales on my abacus, speaking kindly to customers,
practicing greetings in Portuguese, Chinese, Tagalog, and Hawaiian.

Harm is the opposite of what we practiced
and there is no enmity within us, only regret
we cannot be seen except as a race enemy to yours,
our blood our crime, our innocence already cause for conviction.

Go take your photographs, I say, go show me in handcuff
with soldier dey go shove me from behind with the barrels of their guns
so you can see how the military takes action against Japanese
who are too far away for soldiers to fight, their ships too small
against the horizon on the sea to matter in the gossip of your people
who are so frightened now, the spectacle that is my calumnious
arrest might calm their vicious hearts greedy for reprisal.

BALLAD OF BELVEDERE, 1944

Homage to the 442nd

We stay pin down by Wehrmacht cannon.
From above we say attack dem.
Was one silent march to Kingdom Come—
Had to bushwhack behin' da mountain.

We was one regiment of men
From camp, from sugarfields.
We went go slow and took whole night.
All silence, eh? War come more real.

Went charge da ramparts at daybreak,
Us guys from Company B.
We open fire, shed German blood.
Nazis go fall like leaf.

None alert for sound da alarm.
Dose still alive scatter far.
We take down da swastika flag.
On da castle we went put ours.

Over da mountain, in twilight,
Da moon go rise—took watch.
One mortar make da kine flight
Across da sky ju'like one blood splotch.

In one field below da fortress,
We assemble dose still yet get life.
We pass out rations, cigarettes.
Dere faces stay surprise.

Bumbye, it start hard for rain.
More worse, us guys hold watch.
We scared more go'n' come attack,
And *puka* us fresh bloodstain.

Our wounded, our dying, our friends
Call *Namida!* from da wet bunks.
Da sun, da moon go rise again.
Us living give 'em t'anks.

Not many lef' for remember
We fought for prove ourselves.
For funeral we stan' in honor.
Ass how we care each oddah.

T'ousands *make*—we aged few,
Us guys for dem we sing out loud.
From now we stay near da groun'.
Us guys on grass we ju' like dew.

SCARLET PAINTBRUSH

Castilleja miniata grows in dry marshes, open woods, and meadows
In a range from Northern California through Eastern Oregon and the Cascades.
My cousin, just married, came upon a field of them while hiking around Mt. Rainier.
She posted a selfie on Facebook, she and her husband both ruddy-cheeked,
Facing a brisk wind, their hair tousled, making whips like florets of paintbrush
Dancing around coronas of pure happiness visited upon them by the Everlasting.

And, one summer, I saw a field of paintbrush bent by a flat heel of wind
Sent from a black thunderhead scudding over Fish Lake near McKenzie Pass.
They are alive in memory from when I drove to my brother's summer camp
On the southeastern edge of Mono Lake where he trained his string of birddogs.
There were patches of paintbrush popping up along a streambed, dandles of red
Fluttering over dry ground, surrounded by salt beds, tufa, and black lava sands.

In 1944, internees at Tule Lake gathered the blossoms to pound into paste,
A dye they mixed in *chawan* for painting flowers on burlap they'd scrounged
To make humble sleeves for chopsticks they'd fashioned from scrap pine,
A decorous touch at mealtimes while incarcerated during World War II.
Did Uncle Mas tell me this? At 95, the last time he'd visited? Away at college
In Stockton when war broke, he got rounded up by Executive Order 9066.

Over a century ago, in 1873, a shaman made a like paste from paintbrush blooms
To dye the red tule rope he wove for a sacred circle around the Ghost Dance
Of 52 warriors who would make their stand against 400 U.S. soldiers
And cavalry sent to remove the Modoc from the lava beds of their native land.
The rope was said to make them invisible, that their dancing would overturn
The Universe, exiling the whites, restoring a people to where they belonged.

The next morning, a thick tule fog rose from the land, engulfing the crags and trenches
Of the stronghold where the warriors hid, making their movements invisible.
After many days, the Modoc were victorious, the soldiers and cavalry repulsed,

But more came and the medicine of the paintbrush faded, four Modoc were hanged,
And the rest removed to reservations in Oregon and Oklahoma, a scattered people.

My friend, their descendant, retold this story on the deck in back of my house,
Invoking the fragile promise of protection by the paintbrush, the sleevelike florets
Of them inviolate in memory like monks gently genuflecting toward the West
Through the firedamp of grey air and the final smudge of scarlet that was the sun.

AN ODE TO INDEPENDENCE DAY,
LAGUNA BEACH, 2007

> I hear America singing, the varied carols I hear . . .
> WALT WHITMAN

We came like a tide swelling to the shore, except from inland—
places named for saints in Spanish, a realtor's dream, a field of oranges,
and, nostalgically, a town planned for post–Civil War elites
seeking refuge from a Chicago rife with newcomers—
Santa Ana, Lake Forest, Anaheim, and Garden Grove.
Our sleek cars, metallic sharks, cruise the streets and nuzzle curbsides,
steel skins ticking as the air cools in the onrush of the evening chill,
sand and salt in a light haze over insolent, candy-flake paints.
It's the Fourth in Laguna Beach and we've spent the afternoon
strolling the boardwalk from the bluffs to the basketball courts,
past the eponymous hotel and rows of cheap motels with capricious names,
eating over-salted popcorn and lapping our drools of ice cream.

It's almost amnesiac, this dry equinoctial day
fading to fireflame glimmers of light
that burst from all the west-facing windows along the shore,
splashing like a sudden semaphoric spume of a traveling wave
crashing against a shoreline inlet of rocks sculpted slick by the sea,
spilling one season into another, one year into ten,
and my decades of penitential wandering into this single night.

In 1984, still a stranger to this privileged world of beaches,
suburbanites, and their forgetfulness, I cast my ballot
in a spring primary for the candidate of the Rainbow Coalition,
Jesse Jackson, a preacher who'd once stood in shock and outrage
over the Reverend Dr. King slain on a hotel balcony in Memphis in 1968.
Jackson had spoken of the solidarity of peoples,
voice hectoring and climbing in anaphoras and chants
into a stirring oratory I was moved to hear even via television.

His opponents were both drab and toney—Walter Mondale,
a homespun Minnesotan once V.P. and obviously the party's choice,
and Gary Hart, the junior senator from Colorado
with blow-dried hair and a platform of "New Ideas."
Not yet disgraced (that was yet to come, photos
trysting on a yacht, the bikini-clad girlfriend in his lap),
Hart was image-over-substance and espoused only vaguely,
while Mondale skewered him, crying "Where's the beef?"
live and on-camera during a televised debate. The laughs killed Hart,
but I admit I might have gone for the man in the teased hair
except for the preacher who urged us to rally around the suffering,
show our strength joining hands across neighborhoods and races
so we could uplift ourselves above the world as a rainbow does over the earth,
rising in an arc of many colors across beaches, bluffs, and canyonlands.

The next morning, when I drifted back to the polling station
(it was my public library), I'd hoped to see the full tally posted.
I knew my man would not have won the precinct—an entire city—
but I wanted to gauge the showing he'd made in my neighborhood.
There was a long sheet of squash-yellow cardstock
taped to a window of the library annex a half-block away,
and I ran my eyes down to the report line for Lido, #53-075,
my little beachy *arrondissement* highlighted in a trailing spoor of red
from a marker, then circled with a flourish in case you missed it.
There were a hundred plus for Mondale, nearly eighty for Gary Hart,
and even a sprinkling for McGovern in his last hurrah. But there,
starkly, was the number "1" beside Jackson's name—a single vote.
I thought to myself, *How could?*—then realized I was alone
among the sand-footed citizens in this county of white flight,
my values islanding me in a wide sea of beliefs counter to mine.

Yet, now beside these evening throngs who crowd against the barriers
and trample the tough lawns of grass beside the Coast Highway,
I hear a multitude speaking languages of murmur and glee
as a bottle rocket screams a Mexican *grito* overhead
and streaks a trail of sparks and smoke across the ash-grey sky
like a ribboning pathway among the zinc shades of the Absolute.

As the first blooms of light burst in silver showers crackling over the crowd,
their faces upturning like dishes of anemones toward the surface of the sea,
there are cascades of American *oos* and *ahhs* and shrieks I'd have expected,
but something more subtly interfused as I move alongside the bustle
is a staccato phrase of Hindi commingled with a melodious babble I think is Farsi,
sing-songs of Brazilian Portuguese against diphthongs of Vietnamese and Hmong.

I spot a child in a festival dress that seems made of ribbons,
red and bright yellow stripes over a flare of purple satin.
She spins on her heel and weighted spangles dart from her braided hair.
Her mother, dressed more simply in a monochrome silk *sari*
and gold-sequined slippers, gathers her in the shrouds of her arms,
and she blends like a swirl of gaudy paint back into the crowd.

The sky has darkened now, not quite to ink,
as gigantic dandelions of light billow then descend,
drooping downwards like silvered ganja-locks on a sparkling willow tree.
No desire is individual tonight as, through these impromptu rituals,
we have found a gathering commune of amity and celebration
that looks beyond the artificial fires we have produced
toward the true stars of our most humane ambitions:
to laugh aloud and feel welcome as we clap someone on the back
named unlike ourselves—José to Shahid, Maha to Mehran—
that we become the luminous dustfall of new identities,
whorls of efflorescence speckled with the afterimages
of our earnest faces and the charitable lights that lit them.

IV

Turquoise and aquamarine slowly pitching against the limestone cliffs,
and I'm hearing teenage boys whoop and scream as they leap from the jetty
to the cool waters under the lighthouse tower of Port de Cassis.

I'm in France, alone with my desire to praise song and the soft,
                                        inner voice of calm
and mourn the brilliantine waters patchy with indigo, streaks of viridian,
                                and powdered temperas of azurite
under the sub-infinite of Cap Canaille cutting like a cruise ship across the horizon.

A pleasure boat chugs through the slick of channel out to sea,
                        thrumming up a V-wash of wake trails,
while the black shadows of stones look up from the bottom
like the upturned faces of drowned cadavers that refuse blessings of the light.
The angling rock beneath the red-tipped tower of a warning siren
jutting out over the sea to the right of where I sit
                        smoking a Robusto on Camargo's terrace
reminds me of the lava promontory of Lā'ie Point somehow,
            a day over thirty years ago I spent with Kawaharada
conjuring old Hawaiian voyagers who found the islands by star map
                and the prophecies of wind and easterly currents from Tahiti.
We gazed up the shore from Punalu'u past Ka'awa and Kahalu'u,
coconut palms, A-frames and *wiliwili* along the beaches,
and let our hearts wander over the past centuries before to the first landfall
                and paid homage to the first canoe that came by star.

Now, I hear the plosive, soft cannonade of a wave
                                against a hollow in the cliffside
and the ratcheting drone of cicadas among the rosemary
                                        and scrubs of pine around me.
A tour guide's amplified spiel drifts over to me from a boat out at sea,
and the pale zodiac of history murmurs back in a crumple of waves.

My life gathers its pieces in a mosaic of cadmium and regret,
all I've lost in the negative space of my days
a faint warble of diminishment amidst the glories of promise
laid out beneath me like a sail of many colors fallen upon the waters,
furling with every turn of sorrow in faint shrouds of a ghostly current.

It's a hazy day and an onshore wind blows in from off the Mediterranean
                                                  in Aeolian puffs
that billow the straw-colored drapes I've drawn aside for this Dufy-like
view of pleasure craft, Zodiac boats, and double-deck tour cruisers
off to the Calanques and their narrow bays of glittering Byzantine blues.
A battered fishing dinghy and what looks like a Chris-Craft nearly collide
                                                  in the channel,
and I can only consider the solace of waters shading from celadon to cyan.

It's a better discipline than calculating my equity balance on May 28, 2005,
than rowing in a flat scull cutting past the fearful prow of a dread future.
Seagulls peep like Erinyes wearing white linen suits, sky-jockeying
                                    and sailing in the greying zenith of woe.
I'm just a dharmakāya short of True Enlightenment, my Self and Soul
                              paralyzed between Bardo and the blues. . . .

What would the Householder of the Azure Lotus say
                        about my life without consolation?
Issa about my having lost nothing but the dew of morning
to the engines of weather, these benign winds of non-change
                                    from the Cyrenaica and Fezzan?

I make a fretful drama of cynosuric worries, the orchestral churn of care
galloping over the currents in my blood like that frantic outboard
on a boat half-past the horizon and too far out for rescue or secure return.

It's too hot to think much about the ochre cliffs of Cap Canaille
or the moan of a tour boat's engines grinding through the aquamarine
                                of the Mediterranean.
I'm inside measuring the width of the white ribboning wake
like a long skin shedding itself from the exoskeleton of a Zodiac boat,
assessing valuations of finitude amongst my household property,
gazing at the bathers as they take turns diving off the limestone promontory
                                below and to my left,
lazily frog-kicking through the cerulean waters of Port de Cassis.

Their bodies are pale as salamanders as they scoot through
                            the zaffre and viridian
back to the rock-toothed shore where they pull themselves up,
amphibian-like, stunning the air with their glistening bodies.
It is a sensate joy that releases like ecstatic vapor
                    from off their skins and sea-drenched hair.
A hand has touched them and *pass'd over their bodies,*
                       but not over mine.

If I were to walk a serrated shore, worn by wind and the idylls
                            of companionship,
I'd be twenty again and arrogant as Icarus
                     making survey of his father's domain,
scanning the surface of the sea for a boil of sardines
                       glinting like a scatter of coins.
Preposterously, I'd glance neither to my left or to my right,
and launch myself straight into a dive of my own,
unshowy and silent as I cut the immaculate waters,
joyous only in the theater of my own being, alone
as the brown salts that dry on the stoic, limestone lips of the sea,
unconsecrated by touch, the liquidinous mask of my face
submerged and upturned, trailing shrouds of sapphire and indigo.

PASSION FRUIT

Passiflora edulis, var. *flavicarpa*

As many times as I've drunk the pulp-flecked, almost clear juice
or imagined the sweet ichor of its essence distilled
into an elegant schnapps sipped onstage by bluesmen, linen-clothed,
their Dobro strings slackened to a loose

key, I'd never seen its gargantuan flower
until a close-up came in a Facebook message—
Blind-boy, Look, it's liliko'i from my backyard—and something edged
up next to me, an ascent through inner phloem, a puzzling power

of a thing, reaching from that tendrilous explosion,
starburst of pea-green floats, constellations
within a god's-eye of purple shadow thickening into lashes
                                        darkened with mascara—
this *passiflora edulis,* var. *flavicarpa.*

Glamorous vibratos of color, consumed within intricacies of a cake-white drizzle . . .
I was sent galloping in purple tangles, my skin scarified on the fine teeth of vines,
drunk with its gleaming, yellow goblets, Polynesian isles
in a garland, forgetting all the times

trunk and limbs were a chiastic hive for bees bouncing in rhythm
                                        amidst green thrashes,
clenching in the throat of a white moon, a silky ooze
on all the cupped flowers of the earth, passions
a white blaze of solitude. Drenched mash of purple dews,

you beguile no one except who drinks of your radiant hymns,
your oyster pulp tinged with magentas of gladness, who hears
that morning glory voice, your loosestrife of madness, your ivory strings
strummed to a jasmined noise that drips colorless tears through tropical air.

A far schooner's white tri-sails dragging across the lip
of a rocky beach at the foot of Cap Canaille's dread bluff,
blue haze in the laden air, the murmurous lapping of waves
                                        against the cliffside,
and the omniscient *chuck-chuck* whir of cicadas
                    shaking their maracas of gladness through the rosemary . . .

I'm out on the terrace at Camargo,
under the latticework and feathery shadows of its reedgrass awning,
hoping for nothing to come—not Sartre's, but Dōgen's—
that this easeful forgetfulness might stretch farther
                                        than the seamless pantalons
of the recumbent sea, than the pale,
blue sombrero of a twirling,
                    mariachi sky.

LITTER FOR THE TAKING

My dream life started in L.A.'s concrete world,
a cityscape of cheap apartments and palm trees,
crowned asphalt streets, blacktop playgrounds aswirl
with immigrant, Black, and Asian kids, a wheeze
of asthma in my chest, missing Hawai'i
and my playmate cousins, the sighing seashore
that had, in foaming curls of white stories,
given a pastoral and all its lore
to paint my daydreams, vanish distress,
and bring back the lost words of pitching waves,
itinerant sellers of *kūlolo* and fish,
evenings of porch music and windward rains.
I had these the way Muir had his Sierras,
a splendor alive in all my waking,
a green mural of folded cliffs, plumeria
blooms on patchy lawns, litter for the taking.

Throughout childhood I had my secret place,
a splendor of mind amid urban squalor,
palimpsests of imaginings to trace,
while a car wreck screeched from the corner.
I conjured yellow *hau* flowers, tofu shops,
fishhooks baited with pink shrimp in waters
tumbled from mossy stones, slate bells of clouds,
the rippled silk of tradewinds in blue tatters
woven across a lagoon's upturned face.
A shut-in, latchkey kid, after school,
I made games of cardboard, string. A sheet of foil
was a silver pond where white egrets raced.

I've since taken survey of other lands,
parades of volcanoes, museum halls.
I lived for pleasures that came to hand
the way sea-run fish school by a waterfall.
I learned of purple wines and their *terroir*.

I gathered postcards at a stop-and-go.
I hiked along a narrow road one summer
chasing the ghosts of Sora and Bashō.
Another, my daughter ran on cobblestones
down a winding, Kafka-esque street in Prague.
Alarmed, just five, she'd found herself alone
while I strolled ahead, my mind in a fog.
It moved back, at work on a fantasy,
something to do with Florentine lunettes,
or a late spring snow at Kinkaku-ji,
a lace-chain of smoke from a cigarette.
Imitations are what I'd sought, innocence
I had as though a child's—a saint's chorus,
unageing wonders taken from guide books
that might beguile and blaze to magnificence.

A copse of oaks, a lawn of fallen, umber leaves
are refuge, my home is now my nation—
walls of Chinese art, rugs of Turkish weave.
I'm content with quieter intimations.
What do I do these days of idleness?
Fugitive thoughts pitch up, the mind's coronas—
an affair among redwoods in Inverness,
a summer shower, ponds gold-lit in Laguna—
from memory, phantoms and their auras.
It's as though I took a road up-mountain
through fog for watercress near Waimea,
Wham! on the radio, then steady rain,
while I dreamt an image, an idea
that gave a moment's comfort when it came.

V

THE SURFACES OF THE SEA

I. TO IDLENESS

It's a humid, breezy day in Cassis, edge of the Mediterranean,
turquoise and cobalt surfaces of the sea
        tumbled with soft laces of waves
curling in towards the tan, cliffrock shore below me.

I'm back again, Cap Canaille's chameleonic cruise ship
                rising over the bay,
flaxen and ochre at the top, midline to water
patchy green with mottles of grey.

Shizuka ni shite the winds command—
    Still the heart—
and I'm starting to want to after years giving voice
to ten thousand pursuits that never speak back,
asking for these twisting arpeggios of quietude.

A catamaran leans left on its white skate,
    tacking in from out there,
a fishing boat trawls its nets half the horizon away,
and I wonder why it's been so hard to find myself
              these long three years of the pandemic,
in streaks of chalk, my profane utterances, and long disquisitions
         trying to explain dark encryptions on the moon
to new initiates, dutiful ephebes in their desk-arm seats.

Don't worry, baby, say those towering Tiepolos of clouds
rising like avatars of white mystery over the cerulean sea.
Yet I wonder why it is we give ourselves to *samsara*
and not the grand Unbeing, that pure void of nothingness,
dona nobis pacem, and an unembittered Emptiness
    out the dross trouble in our souls.

. . . the same sea-soaked air, thrashes of surf against layered rock
                                        hollowed out and wave-tunneled,
the celadon sea-line under a silvery horizon of computer-screen mist.

On rainy days like this, fishermen would be out with their long poles,
bamboo-butted and graphite-tipped, needling the North Shore winds,
the scream of a big bite paying out the multi-colored Dacron line,
and a blalah would leap alert, tee-shirt and shorts flapping,
to grab his rig and set the hook, *ulua* or *pāpio* on the other end
                                        shuddering for the reef.

But here, tourists and locals pad along the concrete path to the lighthouse,
sit in boredom or wonder at its base,
                                witnesses to time present and time past,
            both as likely MIA as present in time future.

Except for that, it's quiet today—no maracas of cicadas in the rushes,
no pleasure or excursion boats pushing from the port to the sea
                                and the Calanques up the coast.
My teen daughter orders up some French jeans, fiddling with her phone
                                        in the dining room,
and I've Hui Ohana on the Bluetooth soundbar, falsetto harmonies
                                praising the bay at Hanalei.

Why have I come so far from the islands that I know?
                    And what do I know except hankering
and the long, nervous trail through entanglement
                        as I gaze up at the invisible river of stars?
What face of mine does the world acknowledge
                                when I call down its rock seawall
for the lost voices of my past to sing through dazzle-throated thunderheads
                                and the warm scarves of rain
spiraling over the sea back to one whose heart roams the phenomenal world
in search of the beginning, finding its abandoned shells, sea-worn luminances,
its vacancies and scornful stares, a shopkeeper's scream *ne touchez pas* . . .

Cap Canaille welcomes me, though, *aloha e* inscripted across its brow
by the wings of gulls, unambiguous, extended across the vaporous distance.
Kaena Canaille, I want to say, *praise the rogue who wanders*. . . .
Home another point up the coast from here and a stage before radiance.

I've a fear of pure poetry sometimes,
> the immaculate peace of it,
so I busy myself in pursuits of distraction,
> looking left and looking right,
> failing to follow the middle path
> away from the burning house of impure consciousness.
I seek illusion but *Thusness*, the true being of the universe, eludes me.
> I fill my days with errands and choring:
> a call to the travel agent, bookings for Paris and Rome.
I test the home alarm, review subscriptions.
> I clean, whirl the Dyson around.
> I Swiffer-sweep,
read the Navien manual why the hot goes cold in the shower sometimes.
> You know the drill.

> And when I check off the whole iPhone list,
I prep classes, reread Theocritus and Virgil,
Wyatt's sonnets, *Lyrical Ballads*, the *Preface* to the Second Edition,
> my notes on the same and more.
> I *delve*. I *seek*.
> I meditate upon thorns of literary pursuit,
its persistence through millennia with variations and filigrees,
> its rarely, *faute de mieux, sui generis* occurrences.

> I create a language of explanation,
> a shining discourse to dazzle young minds,
quoting Benjamin, Longinus, and whomever else I can think of
> from Heraclitus to hip-hop.
I mount Plato's chariot coursing through a sky of the Great Unsaid,
> trailing a luminous stream of revelations as though a comet
> had crossed their songless paths of common language.
I imitate my betters who taught "When I consider how my light is spent,"
> "Sunday Morning," "They flee from me. . . . ," "Taking Leave of a Friend,"
and all the grand stars that light a path for Imagination to follow—
> intimations trailing clouds of glory,
> a skylark, and wild swans at Coole.

Murray the K, Wright and Meyers, Lentricchia,
each bending over books and their binders of loose-leaf notes . . .

A kind of folly, I guess, my effort to follow them.
"Watch yourself," Yusef said to me once back at Irvine,
hearing my ambitions.
He meant, I think, to give more to the quiet of selfless meditation,
the dream-work of dwelling in numinous mysteries and not explanation,
that our job was to make *poems* not poets.

But lately I feel the consolation that these were an unconscious fulfillment
of Kubota's wish to build a school in the sugarlands,
that the children of cane workers might accede to betterment,
that he'd have created, out of goodwill,
a new culture of amity and education.

The war stopped him, his school got shuttered, and he was dragged off
to prison for "sponsoring foreign nationals" by the DOJ,
fearing it was a step toward espionage.
He raged about it all the nights of my childhood.
And I gave him my faithful witness.

It's certain a man can't know *why* things go the way they do,
hot or cold water on his naked skin.
The Book of Changes tells us that.
He can only follow what karma demands,
what the twin wings of his breath sigh he must do—
read the manual, study sutras, chant homage and praise to the heart.

I did this in the dark, not knowing the light of it
till threescore of my old students gathered to meet once,
in Portland, in a nondescript conference room during a convention.
I saw on their faces Kubota's dream for them:
Shaku Shūchi, *Shining Wisdom of the Law* . . .
the tail of the comet that is the human soul
furling in and among them like a banner of stars.

4. SO MANY STARS

I get spidery strands of memory whenever it turns to twilight
                                           and I'm near the sea.
My mind sylphs to whatever lights there are,
                        amber or blue hummingbirds of luminance,
        sparks and buzzes from insect-zappers,
                        a string of candle-flame bulbs
that hang in a bellied loop, post-to-post,
                        along a storefront awning
                                or on the quai
like the one below my second-story, sea-view window
                        here in Port de Cassis.

        70s disco music drifts up from the bistro
                        on the harborside of the long breakwater,
nasal Francophone covers of Earth, Wind, and Fire or Kool and the Gang,
        but then come flagged notes of another tune,
                        bossa nova this time,
                                suggestive as gentle rain,
        a gauze against the purple night,
                Cap Canaille an indigo Leviathan
                        breaching the Tyrian sea.

        I hear it but can't make words out,
                        lyrics sung in French,
                yet the melody so familiar,
its English just beyond my kenning,
                stranded between languages and near a lifetime,
                        the night so clear,
I can see the river of stars stream in a silver banner
                        across the mauve dome of sky.

        On a night like this, my daughter, all of five,
                ran across a pier in Tuscany
        to me at the railing
        looking out over the bay,
                beginning a stray remembrance.
We'd just had dinner.

She'd found a gelateria, and music,
                              piped and programmed,
came from speakers strapped to rusting lampposts
                              along the walkways of the pier.
    The tune was the same. . . .

            Even more years back, sitting on sling-swings
                              on the beach at Hermosa,
        a girl and I were nineteen,
                    talked of being and becomings to one another,
Heideggerian dreams of bringing forth the non-Emptiness we felt
                              within our impatient hearts.
                    I intoned phrases of poetry
        while her own thoughts she kept masked.
                              I spoke too fast.

        And, before that, we were on a splashy date,
                              learning love at sixteen,
    Greek Theater in L.A., a Brazilian group on stage,
                    its lead singer, a contralto,
                        stepping out front for her featured song,
            her dress aflare in bronze sequins,
                    brown hair spilling over her shoulders,
        shifting as she sang under the spangle of stage lights,
                    her dress shimmering like hammered gold.

        And ten years after that, it was a winter night,
                    our pit of a home town,
    the two of us holding each other by the shoulders,
                    foreheads together,
standing beside the pulsing waters of Wakako's backyard pool,
                    ponds of our clothes brimming around our bare legs,
    her taut body within the desert cold
            shivering against mine in a passion held too long,
                and above us,
        in the amplitude of light years,
                    so many stars. . . .

It's a blowsy, *balayage des nuages* day, the sky mostly slate grey
and the sea its deep turquoise to scalloped savoy,
then cool blue under the independence of the horizon.
I try closing windows against a spatter of rain,
curtains interfered with by Aeolian puffs of wind,
and a squid-ink streak of strato-cumulus ruptures
                                             the ultramarine belly of sky.

Off in the hills above the village, a truck downshifts its gears,
descending through a street of quaint and toney shops,
making its daily delivery of charming rags and trinkets.
Nothing else about that I can see, all is shuttered and shooed away,
tables and chairs of beachside bistros pulled back inside
                                             behind draw-down metal doors.

It's maybe like December 8th was, the day after Pearl Harbor,
when my grandfather Kubota shut all his doors and windows
against the coming onslaughts—fury and misjudgment,
guilt-by-race, guilt-by-lantern-light, torching for *kumu* his crime,
guns and ammo he sold in his store the evidence,
short-wave radio, pistol, and dictionaries all confiscated.

FBI telling I one spy for Japan, he said to me most every night
I was ten, eleven, then twelve, Four Roses tinkling with ice
in a jelly jar cupped in his hand. *I no can explain I fishing nighttime.*
No signal submarine me. You go tell, learn speak good, tell my story.

He spent three years in lockup in the stockade,
                         Leupp Trading Post, Navajo Nation,
and I sit free for his sacrifice, for his loneliness and pain,
noting the trembling of winds, the hush of clouds descending
like a counterpane over the unmade bed of the Mediterranean Sea.

Survivor's guilt? Not me.
                         It's homage I pay, mortal to the Titan
learned in ideograms and calligraphy, in chant and sage smoke,
his desk shelf cluttered with Confucian texts and sticks of incense,

Kubota thereafter searching lifelong for the solace his heart and time
                                                could not compose.
Letters were his fire, the idea that eloquence
could ransom innocence for guilt in the registry of history,
his anguish a fuel for my learning, *speak da kine*
                                as though I were a senator.

Make FBI b'lieve I tell the intimate bluff of Cap Canaille,
write Kubota's story on the time-soaked ledgers of its lithic pages.
I tell it on the mountain behind his home village on Oʻahu's North Shore,
its volcanic cliffs rising over cattle lands, once green
                                        with waves of sugar cane.

I tell it to myself—and you, Pilgrim—
                                that we might reach out
and catch the winds of absolution in the empty cups of our hands,
drink in comity the raw ichor of time's truth and righteousness
given to us as we grieve the lost—ones we can name
                                and ones we cannot,
wheeling above the clouds in the turning verses of heaven's stars.

6. ON EMPTINESS

The T'ang Chinese did it best, a poet's solo
               in progressions gathered from wilderness,
while he stood beside the long, vertical scroll of a cataract
                             hung by a natural god,
           its script the Heraclitean flow of the Way.
Or sitting on mats at tea with a friend and fellow bureaucrat
posted on borderlands far from the capital of their educations,
        the two of them engaged in brisk repartee,
                     citing amiably from *The Book of Songs*,
        their light banter a fellowship of *otium*,
             the lyric axis of contemplation,
    while the world persists awhirl in famine, regional war,
                      or harvests of plenty.

What they took from one another, gazing at the festival moon
            as it rose over crags of mountains,
        the slithers and fountains of rivers
                surrounding their hut, ten-foot-square,
        was a joyous loyalty to reflection,
a stilling of the mind that invites the soft thoughts
              of an unknotted wind,
        caravels of contentment with the Grand Whatever. . . .

Let it be was not to them a credo, but daily practice,
           a hermeneutics of calm retreat
like those aquamarine waters below my window today,
        only ripples and whorls like sapphire fingerprints
and ephemeral wings of *bleu de France* upon the sea.

In *M*A*S*H*, the colonel in command fly-fished a trickle of stream—
       the middle of the Korean War—checked out and privileged
to pull a wineglass and bottle of Chardonnay from his creel.
       Did he have it right?

A firecrest chitters, cicadas claxon in waves,
       clicking their thoracic chambers of amplification,
and an excursion boat's engine drones on through the harbor,

trailing a long wake of immaculate lace over the channel's
                                        Persian-blue table.
        The slate sea fills my window and I can see the horizon line from here,
                        the white palette knife of a sail just below it,
                and I wonder if the pale flamingoes of Camargue
                        might present themselves to me someday. . . .

        Why has this lesson been so hard to re-learn all these years,
                why have I allowed the settled law of my soul to be disrupted
                        by tyrannous magistrates of the everyday,
                a groundswell of incessant woe flushing
                                a salty tincture of gentian through my mouth,
my head constantly hung like a seabird hunched before its dive
                instead of lifted to meet the new day's yellow light?

                I've strong espresso in the morning,
and some kind of warbler makes its melodic cry outside my window.
                I can't see Africa from here,
        but I can feel its continental drift,
                a steady tumulus of soul-making,
arising from perigee and about to cross the expansive idylls of ocean.

If only I could stand the infinite measures, wait long enough,
                                and not waste their buoyant resolve.
If only I might dwell in Emptiness the rest of my days.

Prefigurations of fulfillment lie in wait for us,
timeless in their abeyance, then burst as sunshowers
streaming through a cloudbreak unexpectedly, without warning,
the future contained within every one,
not the malediction we once feared,
but an apparition come to save us from our folly.

The indigoed night precedes the hydrangea blue of day.

The Greeks identified and named it *eidos*,
the abstract that informs the living matter of life,
schema its outward shape, the imprint of a ring's seal on wax
as Dante says in *Purgatorio*, *figura* the Latin for them both,
"more plastic and radiant," Auerbach writes, surveying the classics
from his faculty office "with its turquoise views of the Sea of Marmara"
(another scholar wrote) at the University of Istanbul in 1937,
just a touch after he left Marburg, fleeing the Nazis.

Lucretius saw it too, from deep in the watery grave
that was his worry over the terminus of death,
a figment of words, model to copy, the Ideal to its imitation,
a dream image of fancy, the ghost hovering over the Real
like an osprey hunched over in midair, spotting its prey,
a white flash finning under translucent waves.

It floats, Lucretius says, an insubstantial membrane
peeled away from the incarnate world, and Auerbach cites
the example in Virgil when the wraith of Aeneas,
sent by Juno, appears before Turnus, his rival for Latium,
luring him away from battle to the safety of his ship,
shaming Turnus almost to the point of suicide.

Then it was Ovid, Auerbach writes, who first described *figura*
                              as multiform, changeable and *deceptive*,
obscure items in our past living in the murk of insinuation.

Dream figments, they are metonymic atoms, Quintilian says,
whirling in memory around the hidden center revealed only
to the retrospective mind, gazing past ornament to the obscure
(the sun's brief, tentacled flash of viridian at dusk
                quenched in the tattoo blue shades of night).

Joshua *announces* Jesus, said the Church fathers,
Auerbach reading deeply in a rich library of early Christian texts,
noting from Tertullian that *figura* is "something real and historical,"
anticipating another thing equally real and existing in its own time,
seen by its similitude, "the like that is like the like,"
says Wright, my own teacher, California dreaming . . .

It is concrete, a thing that once lived,
Augustine tells us, fulfilled in a moment
when the intellect and the spiritual work as one,
logos the light that shines upon the *eidolon*
as it rounds the bend behind the supermoon
that had once screened it from our sight,
shining forth now from the shadows of prophecy,
the latent form bursting forth in its pure eternality . . .
      His Providence . . . knows no time . . .
already fulfilled by God even as it had remained
                hidden and incomplete to man.

Once in the Afterlife, Cato of Utica, forehead illumined by stars
as Dante describes him, first canto of *Purgatorio*,
serves as guardian at the foot of the island mountain
(so like Hawai'i in its rise from the sea
        to purple banners of clouds in the Empyrean),
his figure lifted from its earthly state
where he was pagan, Caesar's enemy, and a suicide
who should have been in Hell's 7th circle,
              bleeding in the grove of fire,
were he not transposed, via Dantean eschatology,

to the highest Good—*ben dell'intelletto*—

in the poet's vernacular.

Pilgrim in his own story, Dante is startled
to see Cato saved, but, in having chosen death
rather than serve the earthly world rife with sin,
the living man showed true virtue
and was a prefiguration of eternal freedom,
the soul liberated from vile compulsion.
Cato in Purgatory, therefore, empowered by earned authority,
can command Dante to be cleansed of earthly dust
and girded by the reeds of humility,
the poet's tunic belted and knotted by intricate means,
sending him on his way to fulfillment in the higher circles.

In our own lives, far lesser in splendor and dread,
we've mysterious shadows, our faint lights
without meaning,
until we see them again, transformed but harking back
to premonitions
that have been wandering like a fisherman's glass floats
untethered from the frayed netting that is our past.

It is so in the thread of metaphors that stream unseen
by the conscious mind,
as a brook in the city,
discounted, mostly underground, and anomalous.

Deep in Watts, I once entered a two-car garage,
pulled up its heavy spring door, and felt heat
as though Cerberus had leapt upon me,
slathering me with his rough and heavy tongues,
breathing exhaust from the inner fire of his gigantic body.
I gathered myself, saw neat rows of folding chairs
arranged in split, symmetrical banks
before a podium sashed in white satin,
and an altar before the crucified Christ on the far wall.
A huge bible lay on the podium, open to *Acts*, I saw,

and guessed the preacher's sermon-to-be (or sermon-past)
concerned the Old Testament as a shadow of things to come,
the promise of Christ that was Moses,

                                    the Messiah hidden, not in rushes,
but in the prophetic meaning of ancient, Judaic scripture.

I walked forward to a white-washed box
on the right hand of the sacrificed Son of God,
flipped its latch, opened it, and read the meter's small dials,

                                                doing my job.
I closed things up and went back to dirty streets
                            cramped with spillage from garbage cans,
to black angels of gnats in a peppery cloud around my head,
the city seething in flies and resentment all around me.

Or at twenty, in Kawela, the bowl of lagoon brimming before me . . .
Reading Joyce and Stevens and Kawabata on the incline of beach,
the throw from a wave shooting a rope of seafoam at me,
blithe and stupid silly to be back, plotting my path under coconut palms,
living in present tense for a future rose of light in letters and learnedness.
What did I know but earnestness, my acts of study
living in shadows of a long prefatory,
acolyte to a message a flight of seabirds made
with the ambiguous motions of their wings?

What did I know of Kubota and his sacrifice,
of the great-uncle, my adopted ancestor, *kanaka ʻōiwi,*
who ran into cane fire to kill himself before the *luna*s could?
He'd cut a Scotsman's throat with a machete, the story goes,
and would not accept death from any judgment but his own.

Do all our prior generations prefigure us,
the same glance shining forth in each successive face,
ancestral lights we dream scattered and surrounding us,
in passing, one odd fall day in Columbia, Missouri,
at a lamp store we happen to be browsing, naively,
only to burst forth in fulfillment in the speckled cloud of lights,
prisms and floating spores of suns pulsing and collapsing

around us as we rise quickly from a hospital bed
to embrace our newborn child, her head twisted and craning to meet us,
led by recognition of our joyful cry free in air now
no longer entombed in the aqueous cave of our womb,
our own blood rushing heart to head in a starburst of revelation,
all the family faces hung in sheets of an aurora gladdening the artificial air?

Or, in winter, Coleridge attending to the tiny stove of his cottage,
while the white feathers of frost slowly accrete, lathering his windows,
his child asleep in a cradle beside him as he stokes the fire,
witnessing the little *stranger* of flame licking at the grate
(like a schoolboy at the window eager for the lesson's end
and his release where the village green outside awaits),
a luminous imitation of frozen lace, a whip of frost at midnight,
the lashes of his sleeping child, the wick of his Imagination.

When we glance back, we see, as Wordsworth did,
the past in streams and green meadows of the Wye,
in the rise of plenty that comes from a memory bestirred,
the revisitation from that which, once in shadows,
arrives glorified by the numinous power of recognition,
Lacan's purloined letter of Poe's story still on the mantel
but now revealed as the crucial clue risen to discovery by thought;

Or, an event at twenty-two, as one who hears over his page an elder,
intoning lines of strophic praise for autumn or a nightingale,
and realizes, forty years later, standing before a glass case
filled with tiny notebooks, a pocket watch, and note cards
at the Keats House in Rome, near the Spanish Steps,
near Bernini's fountaining boat of stone, that the man
was giving what Keats bestowed upon Cowden Clarke—
the aural memory of majestic poetry read aloud by a master.

Metaphor is a silver chain, a surreptitious trace
just under the surface of the sea of words we founder in,
a separate message we make without thinking to,
the diver's swell and slipknots of airy bubbles
                              announcing him as he ascends.

A white cabin cruiser backs out of the harbor at Cassis,
the crinoline of its wake furling on the gentian waters,
and a drift of small talk spumes up from the terrace below,
scholars and artists foreign to Camargue titivating by the sea.
The sky is powder blue, UCLA colors, at the horizon,
shading darker as it climbs to a zenith of near azure.
Waves ripple, hurried by a light wind *in from Africa*,
as Joni Mitchell sings, soft curls without froth or flotsam,
no seawrack or seaspawn I can wonder on,
Whitmanic surmisals over windrows of seagrass
(and *the beautiful uncut hair of graves*) denied me.

But casting back is what I do, recall the lagoon at Kawela
and its fresh, underwater springs of promise
rippling across the sandy bottom like a curtain of light,
remembering Hayden, remembering the story of Matsuo,
Pine Boy, a foundling child rescued from under ironwood trees
at the end of the military road leading away from Kahuku.

I turn things over, rocks in a stream feeding the McKenzie,
and see the black Balrogs of imagoes to come,
caddis flies coptering, then ovipositing in brilliant waters,
the future in wraiths that cling to stone,
squiggles and nymphlike prefigurations,
emerging umbras of *what-is-to-be*.

The past, even the trail of words we write in a notebook,
does not evanesce but abides as immanence within a universe of *figurae*,
visionary signs that can be read, as Auerbach has taught,
if only we took the moment to and see likenesses therein
insinuating themselves, unborn ghosts of a future meaning
become material in radiant awareness even as we ourselves
are ready to depart this earthliness and join them,
prophetic phantoms about to be rescued from abandonment,
the kindest mother reaching for us, swaddled in boughs of pines.

I sing for clouds, constant rains, a fern chorus
of things forgotten, gingerflowers
of sadness my mother bore, enormous
hollows of the family's past, my father

the dutiful son come to run the store
by the volcano, called by his father
promising a new life, its open door
that swung shut after barely a year.

They left, me still a newborn in their arms,
wailing in complaint for the swift travel,
headed to Kahuku, the new truck farms,
old plantation, and its steel sugar castle.

I grew to six there, a boy barefoot
on dirt and gravel roads, green temple moss
by the graveyard. There were shorebirds in suits
of slanting rain, a grey-brown surf pebble-tossed,

not fit for swimming, a tired sandspit's drift
that marked the margin of all our dreaming.
And what was that? The green folds of cliffs
chanted our imagined names, caught winds heaving

an ocean of clouds that piled like seawrack
muffling the mill's whistle, windrows of rain
gathered upon the mountain's emerald stacks,
the black crown of the day's celebration.

Hidden within the sighing sugar cane, here
I first raised my voice in harmless praise.
I lifted my eyes to the moon's white sphere
And sang a song I hoped would bless all my days.

Notes

Prologue: "I Got Heaven": "My Girl" by Smokey Robinson and Ronald White, as recorded by the Temptations, 1964.

"Under the Oaks at Holmes Hall, Overtaken by Rain": Commemorative poem, Pomona College Student Union Fountain, 1999.

"Reading Miguel Hernández in Bert Meyers' Library": Miguel Hernández (1910–1942) was a Spanish poet and soldier who served on behalf of the Second Republic against the fascist army of Francisco Franco. He was captured and died in prison but not before writing "Nanas de la cebolla," one of the greatest poems of the twentieth century.

> Bert Meyers (1928–1979) was the self-educated and brilliant imagistic poet who first mentored me in the art and whom I wrote about in "Cello," a chapter in *Volcano: A Memoir of Hawai'i*, 1995. His work is collected in *Bert Meyers: On the Life and Work of an American Master*, 2023.

"On a Photograph of Civil Rights Demonstrators": Memphis Sanitation Workers' Strike, 1968.

> "A Change Is Gonna Come" by Sam Cooke, 1964.

"The Night's Cascade": *The Dream on Monkey Mountain* by Derek Walcott, produced by the Center Theater Group, Mark Taper Forum, Los Angeles, 1970.

"Self-Portrait: Just My Imagination": "Just My Imagination (Running Away with Me)" by Norman Whitfield and Barrett Strong, as recorded by the Temptations, 1971.

"After Workshop, Late Fall": MFA poetry workshop, UC Irvine, 1979.

> "I Can't Help Myself" by Holland-Dozier-Holland, as recorded by the Four Tops, 1965.

"Homage to Michael S. Harper at the Equinox of Heaven": Lawson Fusao Inada, Vern Rutsala, and Harper were roommates while they attended the Iowa Writers' Workshop in 1962.

> "Dear John, Dear Coltrane" by Michael S. Harper, 1970.

"Watching Turner Classics with Stanley Crouch at the Hebrew Home, Riverdale": *Double Indemnity*, directed by Billy Wilder, 1944.

"Orison: February, Eugene, Oregon": "Dancing" by Al Young, 1969.

"A Garland of Light": "Ode to a Nightingale" by John Keats, 1819.

> "Those Winter Sundays" by Robert Hayden, 1962.

"At the Grave of Antonio Gramsci, Cimitero Acattolico, Roma": *The Prison Notebooks* by Antonio Gramsci, 1947.

"Reading Jarman at Shakespeare and Company, Paris, 2017": "The Heronry" by Mark Jarman, 2017.

"Beaches": *Pai 'Ohana v U.S.* ". . . evidence appears to be undisputed that the Pai 'Ohana lived at or near Honokohau beach, in the ahupua'a of Honokohau, which is near the 'Ai'opio fish trap, at least since before the turn of the century." David Alan Ezra, District Judge.

"The Other Side of the River" by Charles Wright, 1982.

"Kubota to Zbigniew Herbert in Lvov, 1942": Zbigniew Herbert (1924–1998) was a post-war Polish poet and essayist trained as an attorney. He resisted governmental censorship under Communism.

During WW II, nearly five thousand Japanese Americans were arrested, then held in eight detention centers run by the Department of Justice. These facilities preceded and were separate from the internment camps run by the War Relocation Authority. The former held Japanese American intelligentsia thought to be risks for fifth column activity (spies and saboteurs): Buddhist ministers, Japanese language instructors, doctors, lawyers, bookkeepers, newspaper workers, storekeepers, and other community leaders. These intelligentsia were guarded by Border Patrol agents and U.S. military personnel. Many were not released until after the end of the war.

"Ballad of Belvedere, 1944": Presidential Unit Citation: A, B, and C Companies, 100th Infantry Battalion, 442nd Regimental Combat Team, a segregated unit of the U.S. army during WW II made up mainly of Japanese American volunteers and draftees from Hawai'i and the internment camps. They fought in Africa, Sicily, Italy, and France and became the most highly decorated unit for its size in the history of the American army. The poem refers to their battle on a mountain in Tuscany in 1944.

"Scarlet Paintbrush" is for Don Dexter.

"66": Polynesian star navigation.

"The Bathers, Cassis": "The Swimmers" from "Song of Myself: XI" in *Leaves of Grass* by Walt Whitman, 1855, 1860, and 1867.

"On the Terrace at Camargo": Dōgen Zenji (1200–1253), Buddhist priest and founder of the Sōtō Zen school and author of the *Shōbōgenzō* (*Treasury of the True Dharma Eye*).

"The Surfaces of the Sea" is for Charles Wright.

3. *Apologia Pro Vita Sua:* At a panel at AWP in 2019, former students shared memories of my teaching: poetrynw.org/garrett-hongo-a-tribute/

4. So Many Stars: "So Many Stars" by Alan Bergman, Marilyn Bergman, and Sérgio Mendes, as recorded by Brasil '66, 1967.

"*Figura:* Homage to Erich Auerbach": "Figura" by Erich Auerbach in *Scenes from the Drama of European Literature*, 1959.

There are references to four of my own poems: "Choir," 1988; "Kawela Studies," 2011; "Cane Fire," 2011; and "A Garland of Light," 2019.

"Ancestral Lights" by Deborah Digges, 1985.

"Frost at Midnight" by Samuel Taylor Coleridge, 1798.

"Ode: Intimations of Immortality from Recollections of Early Childhood," William Wordsworth, 1807.

"Seminar on the 'Purloined Letter'" by Jacques Lacan, 1956.

"Carey" by Joni Mitchell, 1971.

[A Child Said What Is the Grass?], "Song of Myself, VI," Walt Whitman, 1855.

Acknowledgments

"I Got Heaven," *Miramar*

"Under the Oaks at Holmes Hall, Overtaken by Rain," *The Southern Review*

"Reading Miguel Hernández in Bert Meyers' Library," *Plume Poetry*

"Sonny Stitt at the Lighthouse, Hermosa Beach, 1970," *Green Mountains Review*

"On a Photograph of Civil Rights Demonstrators," *Salt*

"The Night's Cascade," *The Yale Review*

"Self-Portrait: Just My Imagination," *Provincetown Arts*

"After Workshop, Late Fall," *Cultural Daily*

"Homage to Michael S. Harper at the Equinox of Heaven," *Harvard Review*

"Watching Turner Classics with Stanley Crouch at the Hebrew Home, Riverdale," *Consequence*

"Orison: February, Eugene, Oregon," *New England Review*

"A Garland of Light," *The Sewanee Review*

"At the Grave of Antonio Gramsci, Cimitero Acattolico, Roma," *The Louisville Review*

"*Tanzaku*, Seven Snapshots in Italy," *terrain.org*

"Reading Jarman at Shakespeare and Company, Paris, 2017," *terrain.org*

"Annalena Staring into the Sun, Koaiʻa Tree Sanctuary, Hawaiʻi, *terrain.org*

"Beaches," *Poetry Northwest*

"Watching the Full Moon in a Time of Pandemic," *Together in a Sudden Strangeness: America's Poets Respond to the Pandemic,* edited by Alice Quinn, Knopf, 2020.

"Her Makeup Face," *The Kenyon Review*

"In Marble and Light," *The Sewanee Review*

"Kubota to Zbigniew Herbert in Lvov, 1942," *Poetry*

"Kubota Disembarks the SS *Lurline* in Oakland, January 1942," *The Asian American Literary Review*

"Ballad of Belvedere, 1944," *The Hawaiʻi Herald*

"Scarlet Paintbrush," *Cascadia Field Guide,* edited by Elizabeth Bradfield, CMarie Fuhrman, and Derek Sheffield, Mountaineers Books, 2023

"An Ode to Independence Day, Laguna Beach, 2007," *Harvard Review Online*

"66," *terrain.org*

"Blues with a Feeling, Cassis," *The Kenyon Review*

"The Bathers, Cassis," *The Kenyon Review*

"Passion Fruit," *The Kenyon Review*
"On the Terrace at Camargo," *Catamaran*
"Litter for the Taking," *The New Yorker*
"The Surfaces of the Sea: 1–5," *Literary Matters*
"On Emptiness," *The New Yorker*
"*Figura:* Homage to Erich Auerbach," *The Georgia Review*

I wish to thank all the editors of the above publications for their faith and receptivity.

My special thanks to longtime friends Edward Hirsch and T. R. Hummer for their attention to most of these poems as I composed them. For help with various individual poems, I am grateful to Mark Jarman, David Mura, Alec Stone Sweet, Amy Glynn, Yusef Komunyakaa, Elaine Rubenstein, Andy Lakritz, Peter Morrison, Jeffrey Higa, Russell Shitabata, Jayme Ringleb, and Rick Hilles. Edward Hirsch, T. R. Hummer, and Nicholas Christopher read the entire manuscript and made valued suggestions. Throughout, I enjoyed the constancy and support of Deborah Garrison. *Mahalo nui* to all.

I also owe a debt of gratitude to residency programs at the American Academy in Rome, the Camargo Foundation, Lucas Artists Residencies at Villa Montalvo, and the Lemon Tree House (Camporsevoli, Tuscany) where a number of these poems were first drafted.

In many of my travels, my daughter Annalena accompanied me and filled me with gladness, as she did at home alongside her brothers, Alex and Hudson, and his wife Eve, who together with *hānai* Shelly made for our *'ohana*.

In Eugene, I was sustained and honored by the friendship of Russell Tomlin. *Me ke aloha . . .*

A NOTE ON THE TYPE

Pierre-Simon Fournier *le jeune* (1712–1768) was both an originator and a collector of types. His services to the art of printing were his design of letters, his creation of ornaments and initials, and his standardization of type sizes. In 1764 and 1766 he published his *Manuel typographique,* a treatise on the history of French types and printing, on typefounding in all its details, and on what many consider his most important contribution to typography—the measurement of type by the point system.

Composed by North Market Street Graphics,
Lancaster, Pennsylvania

Printed and bound by Friesens,
Altona, Manitoba

Designed by Soonyoung Kwon